PRO WRESTLING LEGENDS

Steve Austin
The Story of the Wrestler They Call "Stone Cold"

Ric Flair
The Story of the Wrestler They Call "The Nature Boy"

Bill Goldberg

Bret Hart
The Story of the Wrestler They Call "The Hitman"

The Story of the Wrestler They Call "Hollywood" Hulk Hogan

Kevin Nash

Dallas Page
The Story of the Wrestler They Call "Diamond" Dallas Page

Pro Wrestling's Greatest Tag Teams

Pro Wrestling's Greatest Wars

Pro Wrestling's Most Punishing Finishing Moves

The Story of the Wrestler They Call "The Rock"

Randy Savage
The Story of the Wrestler They Call "Macho Man"

The Story of the Wrestler They Call "Sting"

The Story of the Wrestler They Call "The Undertaker"

Jesse Ventura
The Story of the Wrestler They Call "The Body"

The Women of Pro Wrestling

CHELSEA HOUSE PUBLISHERS

Kevin Nash

Jacqueline Mudge

Chelsea House Publishers
Philadelphia

Produced by Choptank Syndicate, Inc.

Editor and Picture Researcher: Mary Hull
Design and Production: Lisa Hochstein

CHELSEA HOUSE PUBLISHERS

Editor in Chief: Stephen Reginald
Production Manager: Pamela Loos
Art Director: Sara Davis
Director of Photography: Judy L. Hasday
Managing Editor: James D. Gallagher
Senior Production Editor: J. Christopher Higgins
Project Editor: Anne Hill
Cover Illustrator: Keith Trego

Cover Photos: Jeff Eisenberg Sports Photography

The Chelsea House World Wide Web site
address is http://www.chelseahouse.com

First Printing

1 3 5 7 9 8 6 4 2

Library of Congress Cataloging-in-Publication Data

Mudge, Jacqueline
        Kevin Nash / by Jacqueline Mudge
            p.   cm.— (Pro wrestling legends)
        Includes bibliographical references and index.
        Summary: A biography of the pro wrestler Kevin Nash, nicknamed Diesel.
        ISBN 0-7910-5827-1 — ISBN 0-7910-5828-X (pbk.)
        1. Nash, Kevin, 1958—Juvenile literature. [1. Nash, Kevin, 1958- 2. Wrestlers.]
    I. Title. II. Series.

    GV1196.3 N37 2000
    796.812'092— dc2
    [B]
                                                          00-020729

Contents

1 THE DIESEL TRAIN ARRIVES

The odds were stacked against him. On April 13, 1994, there was no reason for anyone to think that the man known as "Diesel" had any chance of beating Razor Ramon for the World Wrestling Federation (WWF) Intercontinental title. After all, as several other Intercontinental title contenders had pointed out in protest and complaint, Diesel didn't really deserve the title shot in the first place. Title shots are generally granted to competitors who have proven themselves worthy of the occasion, or to those who have paid their dues. Diesel was a newcomer in the WWF and so far his record was not outstanding.

Diesel, whose real name was Kevin Nash, stood seven feet tall and weighed 356 pounds. His strongest asset in the ring, however, was his killer instinct. Wrestling fans had seen that killer instinct three months earlier at the Royal Rumble pay-per-view event, when Diesel single-handedly eliminated seven men in the unique battle royal: Bart Gunn, Scott Steiner, Owen Hart, Kwang, Bob Backlund, Billy Gunn, and Virgil. When Diesel was finally eliminated, it took three men—with a combined weight of more than 1,000 pounds—to hoist him in the air, hurl him over the top rope, and land him on the arena floor.

Kevin Nash raises the belt and shouts in victory after beating Razor Ramon for his first WWF World heavyweight title at Madison Square Garden on April 13, 1994.

7

Diesel was not only an imposing wrestler, he was also physically intimidating. His right hand punch and clothesline were among the most lethal in the sport.

His record in the ring, however, was only average. True, Diesel had pinned WWF World champion "Hitman" Bret Hart, but only after Bret's brother Owen had interfered on Diesel's behalf. He had also beaten Marty Jannetty and Virgil, but so far he had not matched up well against the federation's elite, such as Tatanka and Razor Ramon, who one day would be known as Scott Hall in World Championship Wrestling (WCW).

Diesel's record in the high-pressure pay-per-view shows was not especially noteworthy. He had lost a tag team match at the 1993 Survivor Series, ultimately come up short at the Royal Rumble, and been left off the card completely at WrestleMania X in March 1994. The message couldn't have been clearer: when you're left off the card for WrestleMania, you're not among the WWF's contenders. Perhaps one day, Diesel would be ready for the big time, but not now.

Besides, nobody could quite figure out what Diesel was doing in the ring in the first place. His reputation in the WWF was that of a thug, not a wrestler.

Shawn Michaels, the two-time former Inter-continental champion known as the "Heartbreak Kid," had brought Diesel to the WWF as his bodyguard a year earlier, rescuing Diesel's career. In WCW, Diesel had been going nowhere fast, first as Oz, then as Vinnie Vegas. The Oz character, a wizard-like behemoth dressed in green, was absurd at best, while Vinnie Vegas's dice had never come up sevens. Nash's career seemed over before it had really begun.

Fortunately, Nash had one thing on his side: his enormous size. When Michaels went looking for a bodyguard, he settled on the biggest, toughest guy he could find. Some cynics in wrestling snickered that he had also chosen the biggest, toughest guy who had no future in wrestling.

As it turned out, Michaels's bodyguard could wrestle a bit, too. However, men who "wrestle a bit" don't win major titles, especially against experienced foes such as Razor Ramon.

Ramon, whose nickname was "the Bad Guy," was in his seventh month as WWF Intercontinental champion. The Bad Guy had scored his most impressive victory on March 20, 1994, when he defeated Shawn Michaels in a ladder match at WrestleMania X. In that bout, the Intercontinental belt was hung above the ring. The winner would be the first man to climb the ladder and grab the belt. In one of the greatest WrestleMania matches ever held, Ramon survived a brutal beating by Michaels, and won after 18 minutes, 45 seconds of all-out, exhausting wrestling during which Diesel never interfered.

That was the backdrop against which Diesel stepped into the ring on April 13, 1994, at the War Memorial Auditorium in Rochester, New York. The arena was packed with screaming fans and the television lights were glaring, but this was no big-time pay-per-view event. It was the second of two television tapings in two nights for the WWF, the latter half of an exhausting upstate New York tour. The night before in Syracuse, Ramon had beaten Diesel by disqualification when Michaels interfered in the match.

For Diesel, this was yet another chance of a lifetime. He knew that just a year ago in WCW, he never would have received a shot at a major title, much less two shots in two nights. Back in WCW, he was hardly a championship contender. He also knew that if he didn't beat Razor Ramon soon, the WWF would stop giving him chances. Although Diesel wasn't in a career-breaking must-win situation, he had reached the point where he had to prove himself as a major player, at least to convince himself, if not the rest of the wrestling world, that he had potential.

Many fans in the crowd that night must have been asking, "If Shawn Michaels couldn't beat Ramon, how in the world can Diesel?" Perhaps Diesel was thinking the same thing as he paced in the locker room before the match. Michaels wasn't wrestling on the card, so he and Diesel had plenty of time to sit down, talk about strategy, and prepare for the match. An important part of their strategy was determining the right moment for Michaels to interfere. In this match, once again, the bodyguard figured to get help from the man he had been hired to protect.

As match time arrived, Diesel and Michaels left the locker room and started the long, slow walk to the ring. Michaels would be in Diesel's corner for this match, just as he had been for most of Diesel's matches. Diesel was introduced first. The crowd cheered, but the cheers were for Michaels, not Diesel. Then Ramon entered the ring to a mixture of loud boos and cheers.

*Fans were awed
by his sheer power
when Diesel single-
handedly eliminated
seven men during
the Battle Royal
at the Royal Rumble
in 1994.*

At 6' 8" and 290 pounds, Ramon was not
about to be intimidated by Diesel's size. Ramon
came out strong from the opening bell. As
expected, the match immediately turned into a
brawl as the two big men tried to tire each other
out. Ramon kept looking over his shoulder,
figuring that at some point Michaels would
interfere. After all, Michaels had interfered in
every one of Diesel's matches against Ramon.
Finally, as expected, Michaels began taunting

Ramon. Within seconds, he had "the Big Guy's" attention.

Ramon was incensed. As much as he wanted to finish off Diesel, there was nobody in the world he hated more than Michaels. Ramon simply couldn't control himself. He had to get his hands on Michaels, and that's when he made an historic mistake. He turned his back on Diesel.

Michaels climbed into the ring. Ramon chased after him. Michaels slipped between the ring ropes and outside the ring. Ramon gave chase. Diesel, too, slipped between the ring ropes and onto the arena floor. Ramon turned around. Diesel kicked him in the face. Ramon was stunned. Diesel got him back into the ring and executed his jackknife power bomb, a devastating finishing maneuver in which he lifted his opponent waist-high, then drove his opponent's shoulders to the mat. When Ramon crashed to the canvas, he screamed out in pain, then lay prone. He couldn't move. Outside the ring, Michaels began celebrating as Diesel closed in on Ramon and covered the champion for the pin.

Three seconds later, the bodyguard, the unlikeliest of contenders, had become WWF Intercontinental champion.

Michaels and Diesel were exuberant. They had successfully accomplished one of the most stunning upsets the WWF had ever seen. Almost as sweet as the victory over Razor Ramon was the victory over Diesel's critics, the ones who said he didn't deserve the title shot. They had finally been silenced.

"I wouldn't want to be in Razor's position now," WWF manager Jim Cornette said at the time. "I always did think he was more lucky than anything else when he was champion. Now it's up to him to beat Diesel, and I don't see that happening. Michaels and Diesel were an unstoppable combination before, when Michaels was champ and Diesel was his bodyguard, and now they are again."

Cornette was wrong. Just five months later, Ramon would get his revenge by beating Diesel for the Intercontinental title. But by that time, Diesel was in the middle of an eight-month long surge that would catapult him to the top of the sport.

The Diesel train had arrived, and it was unstoppable.

2 | TOWER OF POWER

Kevin was born on July 9, 1958. His mother and father, Robert and Wanda Nash, both worked at the Ford Motor Company near their ranch home in suburban Detroit. Kevin had an older brother, Mark, and a younger sister, Kim. It was a working-class family, and a happy one. Mother and father decided that religion was an important part of their children's lives, and made sure the family never missed church on Sunday.

Kevin Nash grew up surrounded by love. There was also a playful side to balance the serious side of everything the Nash children did. Dad played with his sons—toy soldiers, sports, and other games. Church on Sundays might be followed by a trip to a local restaurant, where they'd have a nice family meal. Bath time might find Dad sneaking into the bathroom and pouring cold water over their heads. Today Kevin can still be playful like a child, and he still has a deep sense of religion.

Other than playing with his father, young Kevin had two passions in life: comic books and pro wrestling. The 1960s was the era of Dick the Bruiser, Gene Kiniski, Lou Thesz, Bobo Brazil, and the Sheik. Kevin was fascinated by what he saw on the family's black-and-white TV. There was something about this fantasy world that appealed to him and inspired his

---

Wrestling under the name Steel, Kevin Nash, right, takes a beating from Rick Steiner. Nash began his wrestling career in the NWA as Steel of the Master Blasters, but he and his partner, Blade, frequently lost to the Steiner brothers.

When Kevin Nash was growing up in the 1960s, Dick the Bruiser was one of the most popular wrestlers of the time. Here Bruiser pins his opponent, Larry Evans, during a 1964 match in Los Angeles.

imagination. Like the comic books he also loved, he was watching superheroes working their magic.

Kevin's mother wasn't pleased by her son's fascination with blood and violence. She tried to make him stay away from his Uncle Chuck's house, where Kevin would satisfy his love for wrestling by watching the sport on TV and reading his uncle's collection of wrestling magazines. The appeal of the sport was just too great for Kevin.

Then the fun tragically stopped, long before it was supposed to end. Robert Nash was just 36 years old when he died of a heart attack in 1966. There would be no more toy soldiers and no more sneak-attacks at bath time. For a while,

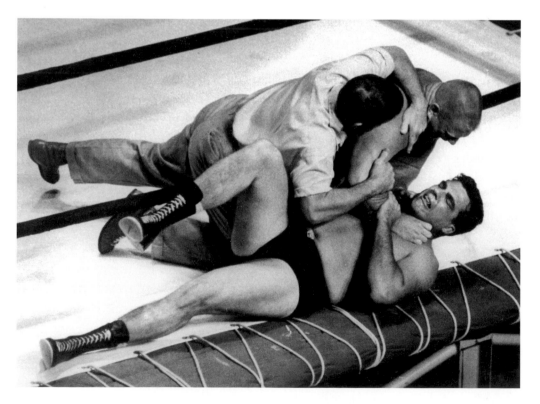

it seemed, there would be no more laughter. Kevin was only eight, too young to lose a father. He still had a lot of growing up to do, but he'd have to do it without his dad.

Kevin's mother, Wanda Nash, had stopped working so she could raise the family. Now she had no choice but to return to work at the Ford plant. She was determined to do everything possible to continue the upbringing that she and her husband had started for their children. Sometimes she worked the night shift, and Kevin and his two siblings would have to stay with a neighbor or a relative. Through it all, the kids were always provided for: they ate, they were properly clothed, and they went to school.

Wanda Nash remarried two years later, and the children were fortunate yet again, because their stepfather was loving, caring, and funny, too. Allan MacDonald became "dad" to the Nash children who soon became heroes of the gridiron, the baseball field, and the basketball court.

Kevin was always a big kid. By the age of 14, he was 6'10", towering above his classmates, friends, and just about every adult in Detroit. He loved wrestling, and toyed around on the mat several times, but he was a natural for basketball. Tall and solidly built, Kevin was also strong and agile. He played his first organized basketball game in sixth grade, and made the varsity basketball team as a freshman at Trenton High in Detroit. He was such a star at Trenton High, nearly 200 colleges and universities wanted him to play basketball for them. He chose the University of Tennessee (UT).

The Volunteers were an outstanding team in the late 1970s, when Kevin played there. In one

By his late teens, Nash was seven feet tall and a high-school basketball star. Recruited by the University of Tennessee, Nash played three seasons for the Volunteers before turning pro and playing in Germany.

of his three years, they reached the Sweet 16 (one of 16 finalists) in the NCAA championship tournament. But things did not go smoothly for Nash at UT. He and coach Don DeVoe did not always see eye to eye. Their problems peaked in 1980 during a game against the University of Kentucky. Nash had been involved in a shouting match with several Kentucky players during the game, and after the game he and DeVoe argued in the locker room. Although Nash finished the 1979–80 season at Tennessee, he did not return for his senior year and left school. Nash took his big inside game to Germany, where a knee injury ended his basketball career at the age of 25, after four professional seasons.

The injury was serious enough for doctors to wonder whether Nash would ever again be able to play sports. With nothing else to do, Kevin returned to Detroit, and got a job at the automobile plant, working on the assembly line. On Friday nights, he and his buddies went out and spent their paychecks on a good time. One Friday night, Kevin and his friends wound up at the Joe Louis Arena in downtown Detroit for a WWF card.

Kevin hadn't seen a wrestling match in years. Watching what was going on in the ring, he thought to himself, "I can do that." He was seven feet tall and weighed 356 pounds. He had a good sense of humor and liked talking, so interviews wouldn't be a problem. Besides, it was either wrestling or the assembly line. The decision was an easy one to make.

Kevin moved to Atlanta and got a job as a bouncer at a nightclub. He didn't know exactly how to proceed on his way toward becoming a professional wrestler, but he figured that Atlanta, one of the capitals of pro wrestling, was as good a place as any to start. While working at the nightclub, Kevin became friends with wrestlers such as Barry Windham, Dusty Rhodes, and Rick and Scott Steiner. They told him about a nearby wrestling school, the Power Plant.

Nash started a new life. His routine found him weightlifting in the morning, working from 11:00 to 8:00, then attending wrestling school at night. Toward the end of 1990, he signed his first contract with the National Wrestling Alliance (NWA), and wrestled under the name Steel. He had an orange Mohawk haircut and teamed with Blade. Together, they were called the Master Blasters.

At first, the Master Blasters did a lot of losing. The competition was too tough; the Steiner brothers, Doom, and the Road Warriors were the dominant tag teams at the time. For Kevin Nash, losing was something he'd have to get used to for a while.

3   THE BODYGUARD

Master Blasters Steel and Blade were big and muscular, they wore colorful face paint, and they looked like something out of the comic books that young Kevin Nash used to love so much. In October 1990, the Master Blasters scored three wins in three nights over more experienced competition. They even entertained thoughts of winning the NWA World tag team title. "We're this close to winning it all," Nash said as he held two fingers less than an inch apart. "Once we start getting those title shots, those belts will be ours. Nobody is gonna hold us back."

Actually, somebody was going to hold them back. NWA promoters were in no hurry to grant title shots to the Master Blasters. The closest the duo ever got to being nationally recognized was on October 27, 1990, when they made their pay-per-view debut at Halloween Havoc and defeated the Southern Boys. It was all downhill from there, and the Master Blasters soon disbanded.

Then two important things happened for Kevin Nash. In 1991, WCW replaced the NWA as the sport's number-two promotion, behind the WWF, and Kevin Nash became Oz.

Millionaire businessman Ted Turner had purchased the NWA cornerstone Jim Crockett Promotions in 1988. It was

---

Kevin Nash took on the persona of Diesel when Shawn Michaels, below, asked him to become his bodyguard.

Unable to convince federation promoters to grant him title shots, Kevin left the Master Blasters behind when WCW replaced the NWA.

christened WCW, and Turner began pouring money into this new federation. Turner also owned a vast library of MGM movies, including *The Wizard of Oz*. WCW promoters decided they'd take advantage of this cross-promotional opportunity by naming their wrestlers after characters in MGM movies.

It was an experimental attempt to draw attention. Since Nash wasn't doing much other than losing singles matches as Master Blaster Steel, he was the first victim of this not-so-grand experiment. As Oz, Nash wore green tights and had his hair dyed silver. He walked to the ring wearing a rubber mask and was accompanied by his manager, Kevin Sullivan, a renowned rulebreaker. Sullivan was called the Wizard.

Oz made his first appearance at SuperBrawl I on May 19, 1991. He came to the ring accompanied not only by the Wizard, but also by Dorothy, Toto, Tin Man, Scarecrow, and the Cowardly Lion. Nash felt like a fool. He had realized from the start that he might have to do some unusual things to make a name for himself in wrestling, but he never thought the road to stardom would be paved with yellow bricks. Despite all of these absurd distractions, Nash needed only 26 seconds to defeat Tim Parker.

At first, Nash did pretty well as Oz. On June 12, 1991, he used a move called a helicopter slam, in which he whirled his opponent above his head before slamming him to the mat, to defeat Johnny Rich in only one minute, 29 seconds. His ring entrances were spectacular. His size was imposing. But he didn't get his first real test as a singles wrestler until the 1991 Great American Bash, when he squared off against Ron Simmons, who would win the WCW World heavyweight title the following year.

The match was no contest. With just under eight minutes gone, Simmons shoulder-blocked Oz, sending him crashing to the mat, then scored the pin. That was the beginning of the end for Oz.

As the losses piled up, Nash wasn't receiving any kind of positive attention. His gimmick was foolish. His wrestling was tentative. He was raw and unproven, and he wasn't getting any chances to prove himself. His confidence

wavered. He appeared on fewer and fewer cards.
At Fall Brawl '91, he was one of the last three
men remaining in a "Georgia Brawl" battle royal,
but was eliminated by El Gigante. At Halloween
Havoc '91, Oz filled in for Cactus Jack and lost
by submission to Bill Kazmaier in under four
minutes.

The fans were booing Oz. They thought he
was ridiculous, and he was doing nothing in
the ring to convince them they were wrong. It
was time for another gimmick. Oz became
Vinnie Vegas. Nash, who got his start in
wrestling by working as a nightclub bouncer,
was now playing the part of a casino bouncer.

Like Oz, Vinnie Vegas got off to a great start.
At Clash of the Champions XVIII on January
21, 1992, he needed only 56 seconds to pin
former world champion Tommy Rich. This time,
Vegas's finishing move was a "snake eyes" face-
drop onto the top turnbuckle. The victory was
so impressive that manager Harley Race
recruited him for his new stable, which also
included Big Van Vader and Mr. Hughes. Race
teamed Vegas with Mr. Hughes and sent them
after the U.S. tag team title. WCW promoters
didn't pay much attention to them and, after a
while, neither did Race, particularly after Vader
won the WCW World tag team title.

Before long, Nash's WCW career completely
fell apart. Frustrated with Race's lack of attention, he jumped to "Diamond" Dallas Page's
"Diamond Mine" stable. At the time, Page was
only slightly more successful than Nash. At
Halloween Havoc '92, Vegas and Page were hum-
bled by the team of Erik Watts and Van Hammer.
Vegas and Page were going nowhere fast. When
Page got hurt, Vegas was forced to go it alone in

singles matches. He lost to Watts and 2 Cold Scorpio, hardly heavyweight title contenders. He was able to beat Tony Atlas in an arm-wrestling contest, but there were no title matches, no big breaks.

Then his contract with WCW ran out.

Although WCW promoters couldn't see the value in a 7' strongman with great athletic skills and a quick wit, Shawn Michaels, the former WWF Intercontinental champion, certainly could. Around that time, Michaels, a cocky rulebreaker, decided he needed a bodyguard. Michaels had lost the Intercontinental

Nash experimented with different characters called Oz and Vinnie Vegas before meeting success as Diesel, Shawn Michaels's bodyguard.

title to Marty Jannetty, his former tag team partner, on May 17, 1993, and desperately wanted it back. Jannetty had Curt Hennig helping him out. Michaels figured he should have some help, too. When he found out that Nash's WCW contract had expired, he called the big man. Although Nash was more interested in being a wrestler than a bodyguard, he agreed to join Michaels in the WWF.

On June 6, 1993, Michaels squared off against Jannetty in Albany, New York, and introduced his new bodyguard. When the bout started, Nash shielded Michaels for several minutes, then took his spot at ringside. After 20 minutes of heated action, Jannetty scored with a dropkick and closed in for the pin. Michaels kicked out, then whipped Jannetty into the ropes. Without the referee's knowledge, Nash tripped Jannetty. Michaels covered him for the pin.

Nash took his new name—Diesel—at the 1993 King of the Ring pay-per-view, where he again helped Shawn Michaels win. Over the next few months, Diesel interfered in matches whenever he had the chance and he helped Michaels gain a stranglehold on the Intercontinental title. He did no wrestling, he just carried out his duties as Michaels's bodyguard. His reputation grew. He was fierce, had a killer instinct, and was perfectly willing to do Michaels's dirty work. He was the difference in Michaels's red-hot feud with Hennig, who had no idea how to deal with the big man who constantly interfered.

In September, Michaels temporarily left the WWF because of contract problems. Having nothing else to do, Diesel returned to the ring.

He defeated "the Brooklyn Brawler" Steve Lombardi before the losses started piling up again. At the 1993 Survivor Series, Diesel, Irwin R. Schyster, Rick Martel, and Adam Bomb lost to the Kid, Jannetty, Razor Ramon, and Randy Savage. Diesel, it seemed, was a much better bodyguard than he was a wrestler.

THE FAST TRAIN TO STARDOM

4

When 1994 began, the man known as Diesel still wasn't sure where his career was headed. Shawn Michaels was once again wrestling in the WWF. Diesel would have to decide if he would remain a bodyguard or work to become one of the top wrestlers in the federation.

The answer came on January 22, 1994, in Providence, Rhode Island. One by one, thirty wrestlers stepped into the Civic Center ring for the Royal Rumble, a battle royal style match in which one wrestler enters the ring every two minutes, and the last man standing is declared the winner. The only way to eliminate a wrestler in the Royal Rumble was to dump him over the top rope.

That night, all eyes were on Lex Luger, Shawn Michaels, and Bret Hart, the three men considered favorites to win the Rumble. But it was Diescl who stole the show.

The seventh man to enter the ring, one by one, Diesel started eliminating opponents: first Bart Gunn, then Scott Steiner, Owen Hart, Kwang, Bob Backlund, Billy Gunn, and finally Virgil. It took three men with a combined weight of 1,000 pounds to send Diesel over the top rope and to the arena floor. Although Diesel didn't win the Royal Rumble, everybody suddenly knew he was a man to be reckoned with.

Diesel, also known as "Big Daddy Cool," poses for photographers in Times Square during a WWF publicity event.

Fueled with confidence from his Royal Rumble performance, Diesel set his sights on winning the WWF Intercontinental title, which was then held by Razor Ramon. Shawn Michaels had failed in his attempts to win the belt from Ramon, most notably in a thrilling match at WrestleMania X, but Diesel wouldn't fail.

Diesel and Ramon, who would later become best friends, met in the ring on April 13 in Rochester, New York. Michaels was in Diesel's corner, and at the end of the evening, Kevin Nash, the bodyguard known as Diesel, was the new WWF Intercontinental champion.

Diesel was hungry for more. Having won the WWF's secondary singles title, he wanted to win the more prestigious WWF World heavyweight championship. As Intercontinental champion, he was sure to get his chance.

When Diesel battled WWF World champion Bret Hart at the 1994 King of the Ring pay-per-view in Baltimore, fans were treated to a classic battle of size against skill. Hart had a huge edge over Diesel in experience and, in the minds of many experts, in talent.

However, the experts were wrong. Diesel dominated the match. When he dropped a sharp elbow into Hart's midsection and went for the pin, another stunning upset seemed to be in the making.

Outside the ring, though, Michaels had gotten into a scuffle with Jim "the Anvil" Neidhart, Bret Hart's former tag team partner. Neidhart slammed Michaels to the floor, then jumped into the ring and clotheslined Diesel. The referee immediately signaled for Hart's disqualification, meaning Diesel was the winner. It was a hollow victory for Diesel, however,

Diesel captured the WWF Intercontinental championship from Razor Ramon, bottom, who would later become his best friend.

since titles can't change hands in the WWF on a disqualification.

Diesel had a lot to be proud of, however. He had lasted nearly 22 minutes with Bret Hart, the reigning world champion, and he had been in control for most of the match. If not for Neidhart's interference, he probably would have won the championship. Anybody who watched the King of the Ring had to know that Diesel was for real.

Over the next few months, Shawn Michaels and Diesel were forced to deny rumors that a rift had formed between them. Wrestling fans and writers, citing Michaels's immense ego, wondered if he could stand the idea that his former bodyguard was now WWF Intercontinental champion, while he had nothing. Just to prove the skeptics wrong, Diesel and Michaels formed a tag team.

On the eve of a Diesel showdown with Ramon at SummerSlam '94, Diesel and Michaels stepped into the ring against WWF World tag team champions the Headshrinkers at Market Square Arena in Indianapolis. When Samu, one of the Headshrinkers, climbed to the top rope to execute a dive, Diesel rolled out of the way. Samu splashed to the mat. Diesel rolled over and scored the pin.

Now the Intercontinental champion was also the WWF World tag team champion, but the best was yet to come. So was the worst.

Tired of Michaels's interference, Ramon had former National Football League (NFL) great Walter Payton in his corner for his match against Diesel at SummerSlam. Late in the match, Diesel held Ramon while Michaels attempted a superkick, the move he called "sweet chin music" because of where his foot made contact. Ramon ducked, and Michaels struck Diesel. Ramon seized the opportunity and scored the pin. Diesel lost the Intercontinental belt.

Rumors of problems between Diesel and Michaels intensified. Nonetheless, Diesel and Michaels continued to defend the WWF World tag team title. In the ring, they were a well-oiled machine, virtually unbeatable. Clearly, though, they were an unhappy duo.

At Survivor Series '94, Diesel and Michaels teamed with Jim Neidhart, Owen Hart, and Jeff Jarrett against Ramon, Fatu, the Kid, Davey Boy Smith, and Sionne. Diesel was outstanding. First he eliminated Fatu, then he pinned the Kid. Less than a half-minute later, he pinned Sionne. Ramon was the only man left for his team, and Michaels wanted to finish the job. Diesel held Ramon while Michaels set up his superkick, and history repeated itself. Once again, Ramon moved out of the way, and Michaels's superkick struck Diesel instead.

This time, Diesel chased Michaels out of the ring and back to the dressing room area. He and Michaels got into a shouting match. The other three members of their team tried to break it up, but the partnership between Diesel and Michaels was over for good, or so it seemed.

The next night, WWF president Jack Tunney declared the tag team title vacant. Again, however, Diesel had other things on his mind.

The wrestling world was seeing a new Diesel. For the first time, the fans were cheering him. Being Michaels's enemy automatically made him a fan favorite.

Three days after the Survivor Series at Madison Square Garden in New York, Diesel faced off against WWF World champion Bob Backlund, a two-time former champion who had once held the belt for four years. Backlund didn't stand a chance against his bigger, younger foe. In one of the most one-sided world title matches in wrestling history, Diesel stepped between the ring ropes, kicked Backlund in the stomach, then executed his jackknife power bomb for the pin. The entire match lasted only eight seconds. Diesel was declared the new WWF World heavyweight champion.

This was an amazing accomplishment. Just a year earlier, Diesel had been little more than Michaels's bodyguard, an underachieving big man whose career seemed to be going nowhere. Now, within eight months, he had captured the WWF's Intercontinental, World tag team, and World heavyweight titles. He had won wrestling's version of the triple crown.

"I would have figured a dozen guys would've won the world title before Diesel," wrestler

Former WWF World tag team champions Shawn Michaels and Diesel face off before their match for the WWF World heavyweight title at Wrestlemania XI.

Johnny Gunn told *Pro Wrestling Illustrated* magazine. "I always knew he was good, but I didn't think he was that good. He either made a dramatic improvement in a short time, or he held back for a long time."

Unfortunately, while the wrestler known as Diesel was experiencing joy, the man known as Kevin Nash was experiencing heartbreak. On December 27, 1994, his mother, Wanda Nash, lost her four-year battle with cancer. She had been his confidante and inspiration, supporting Kevin in almost everything he had ever done. She wouldn't be there to share in his greatest accomplishment, though. His new standing as one of the most popular wrestlers in the world was an experience he would have to enjoy on his own.

The big man stood taller by the day. Wrestling fans everywhere were wearing Diesel T-shirts and chanting his name. Meanwhile, Diesel had become embroiled in a great wrestling drama. Shawn Michaels desperately wanted to get at him, and Bret Hart wanted to regain the WWF World title. Diesel had a piece of what everybody wanted: superstardom.

In a match at the 1995 Royal Rumble pay-per-view in January, Diesel and Hart fought to a draw because of constant interference by Michaels, Owen Hart, Bob Backlund, Jeff Jarrett, and the Roadie. That same night, Michaels won the Royal Rumble, thereby securing himself a match against the world champion at Wrestle-Mania XI.

Michaels was no fool, and he knew he might need some help to beat Diesel. He hired a new bodyguard, Sid Vicious, who took Michaels's corner for the WrestleMania showdown. With

15 minutes gone in a hotly contested match, Diesel accidentally rammed his own shoulder into the ringpost. Michaels, who had been wrestling beautifully, looked like a sure winner five minutes later when he dropped Diesel and covered him for the pin. Vicious had tried to interfere, and referee Dave Hebner had gone outside the ring to prevent him. While doing so, Hebner twisted his ankle.

Michaels had Diesel covered for five seconds, then 10 seconds! Hebner recovered, crawled back into the ring, and counted to only two before Diesel kicked out. Michaels was enraged. Suddenly, Diesel had gained momentum. He caught Michaels with a boot to the face, then used his jackknife to floor Michaels and score the pin. Diesel had met another challenge, this time with a little bit of luck on his side.

The rematch was scheduled for the following night at *Monday Night Raw*, the WWF's weekly live television show. Interviewed separately, Michaels and Diesel said they had great respect for each other and that they had a hard time concentrating during their match at WrestleMania because they kept thinking about their prior friendship. Michaels even said he was going to give Vicious the night off. After all, Vicious's interference, and his distraction of the referee, had cost him the match the night before.

Vicious didn't care about that. All he knew was that he wasn't going to be tossed aside just because Michaels blamed him for the loss. He called Michaels "a little punk," then attacked him with three devastating power bombs. After the third, Michaels lay motionless on the mat. Then, much to everyone's amazement, Diesel charged out of the locker room and chased off

Vicious. He was too late. Michaels, badly injured, was taken away on a stretcher.

"I owe Shawn a lot," Diesel said later. "I don't know if what happened tonight means we're friends or not. I knew Sid was bad news."

What happened that night actually meant two things: Diesel and Michaels were friends again—this time as unbelievably popular fan favorites—and Diesel and Sid Vicious were now bitter rivals.

5 | THE OUTSIDERS

The WWF World title was in the hands of a big, talented, charismatic wrestler, and the fans loved it. Diesel's popularity grew even greater after his reunion with Shawn Michaels. "Big Daddy Cool," as Diesel was sometimes called, and the Heartbreak Kid both had personality, senses of humor, and the kind of energy that few other duos could match. But Diesel had something Michaels didn't have: the WWF World heavyweight title. That made him a target of every other wrestler in the federation, especially Sid Vicious.

As the WWF's In Your House I pay-per-view event on May 14, 1995, approached, Vicious was not a happy man. He had never been world champion, and he wanted the belt badly. He also wanted revenge against Diesel.

In a hotly contested match, Diesel retained the title, winning by disqualification. He paid the price for his victory, however. Diesel won after he had amazingly kicked out of a pin attempt following a thunderous power bomb by Vicious. Over the next few weeks, as he continued to wrestle, Diesel complained about pain in his right elbow. It turned out that he needed surgery to remove bone chips in the elbow.

Diesel returned to the ring a few weeks later and teamed with Bam Bam Bigelow, a former foe, to defeat Vicious and

In 1996 Razor Ramon, left, and Diesel took their real names of Scott Hall and Kevin Nash and stormed the halls of WCW, declaring war on the federation.

39

Tatanka. Diesel was on his own the next time he faced off with Vicious. He nearly didn't survive the night.

It happened at the In Your House II pay-per-view on July 23. Diesel put his title on the line against Vicious in a lumberjack match. In a lumberjack match, wrestlers not competing in the match surround the ring. Whenever a wrestler steps or falls out of the ring, the lumberjacks throw him back in.

On this night, the lumberjacks seemed more interested in beating up the wrestlers than keeping the action inside the ring. One of the wrestlers was Mabel, and he was determined to

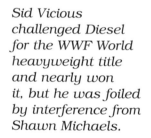

Sid Vicious challenged Diesel for the WWF World heavyweight title and nearly won it, but he was foiled by interference from Shawn Michaels.

make an impact. Early in the match, Mabel pulled Diesel to the arena floor, rammed him into a ringpost, and delivered a legdrop. Mabel weighed 568 pounds. The force of the legdrop stunned Diesel. Then Mabel scooped him up and tossed him back in the ring and into Vicious's waiting arms. At that moment, there was no reason to think Diesel's world title reign was anything but over.

But Diesel had a friend at ringside, too. Michaels entered the fray and stunned Vicious with a flying axehandle from the top rope. Vicious connected with a big boot, then Diesel scored the pin to retain the title.

Diesel was quickly discovering that he had no shortage of enemies. He thought he was making a new friend when he filled in for the injured Lex Luger and teamed with Davey Boy Smith against Mabel and Mo—the team known as Men on a Mission—but he ended up getting triple-teamed by Smith, Mabel, and Mo. Thirteen days later, Diesel gained some revenge by pinning Mabel at SummerSlam '95.

Even Diesel's worst detractors couldn't deny that he had shown himself to be a worthy champion. With the victory over Mabel, Diesel had survived as WWF World champion for nine months and had overcome challenges from Bret Hart, Razor Ramon, Sid Vicious, Mabel, and others. He had proven to everyone that he was one of the best wrestlers in the world. According to *Pro Wrestling Illustrated*, which each year publishes its "PWI 500" rankings of the top 500 wrestlers in the world, Diesel was number one. Shawn Michaels was number two.

Diesel and Michaels were an amazing duo. They appeared to have won the WWF World tag team title in September, only to have the decision reversed by WWF commissioner Gorilla Monsoon. Shortly afterward, Diesel found a new enemy.

This time, he went looking for him.

Diesel was thirsting for revenge when he stepped into the ring against Davey Boy Smith at In Your House IV on October 22. Davey Boy's double-cross a few months earlier was still fresh on his mind, and Diesel saw this not only as an important opportunity to retain the title, but a chance to teach the British Bulldog a lesson.

Smith dominated the match. He neutralized Diesel from the opening bell by working on the champion's left leg to the point where Diesel could barely withstand the pain. Diesel limped around the ring, trying to figure out some way to mount an offense, but he couldn't do a thing. Then Bret Hart, who was working as a TV commentator at ringside, rushed into the ring to attack Smith after Smith had slapped him across the face. Smith was immediately declared the winner by disqualification.

Diesel couldn't believe his eyes. Incensed by a sudden loss that wasn't even of his own doing, Diesel attacked Hart. The two slugged it out, but Diesel couldn't do anything to change the outcome. He was still WWF World champion, but he had lost a chance to punish Davey Boy. "Bret had no right to get involved!" Diesel said later.

The showdown between the world champion and Hart, a two-time former world champion, happened at Survivor Series '95 on November 19. It was a no-disqualification match, meaning the only way Diesel could retain his title would

With his title reign just one week shy of a year, Diesel lost the WWF World title to two-time former champion Bret Hart at the 1995 Survivor Series.

be by pinning Hart or forcing him to submit. The fans didn't know who to root for because both Diesel and Hart were popular.

Diesel was more vicious than he had ever been. He spent the first seven minutes of the match pounding Hart with fists and elbows. Hart fought back by biting Diesel's arm, then concentrating on his left knee. Three times, Hart covered Diesel for pins, but the champion was able to kick out. Diesel caught a break when Hart bounded over the top rope and crashed to the arena floor. Diesel moved in for the kill. Hart tried to climb into the ring, but Diesel kicked him through a ringside table.

Hart appeared to be beaten, so Diesel took his time. He stalked his prey. He slipped between the ring ropes. Hart crawled back into the ring. Diesel signaled to the crowd that he was about to deliver a jackknife power bomb. For all intents and purposes, Bret's title challenge was over.

But Diesel didn't realize that Bret was only pretending to be hurt. As Diesel started to lift Hart for the power bomb, Hart took him down by his legs and cradled him for the pin. After 24 minutes and 42 seconds of unbelievably intense action, the WWF had a new champion.

Diesel's world title reign had lasted one week short of a year. He took out his frustrations by jackknifing Hart twice and hitting three referees who tried to break up the post-match brawl.

"I'm back!" Diesel declared as boos rained down from the rafters of the arena. In the blink of an eye, the most popular man in wrestling had become now one of the most hated.

Diesel was angry not just at Hart, but at everybody, including fans, other wrestlers, and even the people in the WWF who paid his salary. The next night at *Monday Night Raw*, Diesel said he was tired of being the WWF's corporate merchandising puppet. He was going to go back to being the Diesel who eliminated seven men at the 1994 Royal Rumble, the Diesel who didn't care about the rules or the fans.

He was not a man to be messed with. At In Your House V, Diesel was disqualified in his match against Owen Hart for shoving the referee. After the bell, Diesel jackknifed Owen over and over again, even though the younger Hart was unconscious. Diesel got even angrier later in the night when Gorilla Monsoon announced that The Undertaker would get the title shot against Bret Hart at the upcoming Royal Rumble '96 pay-per-view.

Diesel started teaming with Razor Ramon. They were an effective team, winning most of their matches, and began thinking, "You know, we can do great things together."

Shawn Michaels won the 1996 Royal Rumble by last eliminating Diesel. Rather than worrying about Michaels, however, Diesel was more concerned with The Undertaker, who he felt didn't deserve the title match against Bret Hart. The Undertaker dominated his match against Hart and was about to win when Diesel pulled the referee out of the ring. Hart lost the match by disqualification, but held onto the title. The Undertaker vowed to do everything in his power to prevent Diesel from ever regaining the belt.

He made good on his promise at In Your House VI on February 18, 1996. Diesel wrestled Bret Hart in a cage match, in which a wrestler can win by climbing over the top of the cage or by walking through the cage door. Diesel apparently had Bret beaten and was making his way toward the door when The Undertaker tore through the bottom of the mat, grabbed Diesel, and pulled him under the ring.

Suddenly, smoke started spewing out from the hole. When Diesel disappeared, Hart climbed over the cage to win the match. Diesel looked stunned and startled when he emerged from the hole about a minute later.

The wrestling world was hot in anticipation of the rematch at WrestleMania XII. But just when it seemed as if the Diesel vs. Undertaker war might develop into a long-lasting feud, Diesel made a surprising announcement: he was leaving the WWF.

In early March, Diesel told the federation he didn't want to renew his contract when it expired in June. His last day in the federation would be June 6, 1996.

Rumors circulated. Would Diesel sign with WCW? What about Ramon, who had recently been suspended by the WWF for six weeks? Would he, too, bolt from the federation so Diesel and Ramon could continue their budding partnership in WCW?

Before answering those questions, Diesel had some unfinished business in the WWF. His friendship with Michaels came to an end when he pounded the Heartbreak Kid with a chair during a tag team match against Bret Hart and The Undertaker. At WrestleMania XII, Diesel lost to The Undertaker in a furious battle.

At In Your House VII, Diesel and Michaels destroyed any idea that they might reconcile by engaging in a violent no-holds-barred match. Diesel whipped Michaels with a belt and used his power bomb to send him crashing through a table before losing to Shawn after nearly 18 minutes of pure violence.

Shortly thereafter, the wrestling world finally got the answers to the questions it had been asking for months.

Razor Ramon signed with WCW and switched to his real name, Scott Hall. On the day he arrived, Hall warned WCW that he was bringing along two other wrestlers. After all, this was war. For several months, WCW promoters, wrestlers, and announcers had been making fun of the WWF. Hall intended to answer back on enemy turf.

"We're taking over!" Hall announced.

On June 6, 1996, Diesel's WWF contract expired. On June 7, he was Kevin Nash again. On June 16, Nash joined Hall at WCW's Great American Bash pay-per-view card. Hall and Nash said that they, along with a mystery partner, wanted to take on the three best wrestlers in WCW. When WCW executive vice president Eric Bischoff said they'd have to wait until after the card to find out who they would face, Nash and Hall smashed him through the stage. The Outsiders were born.

6 THE END OF THE LINE

K evin Nash and Scott Hall stepped into the ring by themselves at the July 7, 1996, Bash at the Beach. Their
mystery partner was nowhere to be found. Many people
speculated that the mystery partner would be Hulk Hogan,
not only one of the most successful wrestlers in the world,
but also one of the most popular. The idea of Hogan joining
the Outsiders was unthinkable. Hogan was the ultimate fan
favorite.

Nash and Hall were at a distinct disadvantage when the
match began. They were up against three men: Sting, Lex
Luger, and Randy Savage. Nonetheless, the Outsiders dominated the match and injured Luger, who had to be taken from
the ring on a stretcher.

Suddenly, Hogan appeared on the runway and started
walking toward the ring. The crowd cheered, assuming he was
there to help Sting and Savage. Instead, he began legdropping
Savage. Then he high-fived the Outsiders. Incredibly, Hogan
was now a member of the Outsiders.

The Outsiders became the New World Order (NWO), and
the NWO would soon become the most powerful clique in
wrestling history. These men would change the sport. At the
time, the WWF had the biggest following in North America.

*In 1996 Kevin Nash won the WCW World tag team title with his friend
and coconspirator, Scott Hall.*

49

Mostly because of the excitement generated by the NWO, WCW now became the most watched federation.

Nash, Hall, and Hogan were the ultimate bad guys. One night, Hall and Nash attacked Arn Anderson, Marcus Bagwell, Scotty Riggs, and Rey Misterio Jr. with baseball bats. They

At first, Kevin Nash and Scott Hall called themselves the Outsiders. But the Outsiders quickly turned into the NWO, which eventually split into two factions, NWO Wolfpac, which Nash joined, and NWO Hollywood, which Hall joined.

took over the broadcast booth. Nash and Hall helped Hogan win the WCW World heavyweight title. They rammed Luger into a ringpost, causing him to lose the WCW TV title.

WCW was being seized from within, and Nash and Hall were leading the attack. They were enjoying themselves, too. Nash and Hall could barely contain their laughter after costing Luger the TV title.

"That belt meant a lot to our buddy Lex, so the NWO decided he couldn't have it anymore," Nash cackled. "When the NWO puts their mind to something, we get it done."

They were true to their words. The Giant, the 7' 4" former WCW World champion, joined the NWO, followed by Ted DiBiase and Syxx, who later became known as X-Pac in the WWF. Randy Savage also joined the NWO.

Nash and Hall set their sights on winning the WCW World tag team title. They got that done, too, by defeating Harlem Heat at Halloween Havoc on October 27, 1996. They took the belts by force. Nash and Hall stole the cane of Harlem Heat manager Colonel Robert Parker and used it to beat Booker T and Stevie Ray.

Nash and Hall didn't care if they were accused of cheating. They preferred winning by cheating. They thought it was more fun. Even the way they walked was filled with attitude. They took their time. The way Nash and Hall saw things, the world could wait for them.

The NWO got even stronger when WCW vice president Eric Bischoff joined the clique. With this inside man, the NWO was in position to take total control of WCW. As the new year began, wrestling fans wondered, "Would WCW survive 1997?"

Thanks to Bischoff, the NWO was surviving quite well. Nash and Hall appeared to have lost the tag team belts to Rick and Scott Steiner at the Souled Out '97 pay-per-view, but Bischoff ruled the victory invalid because the wrong referee made the three-count. Of course, Bischoff had the right to do whatever he pleased—he was still the vice president of WCW. Souled Out was the NWO's pay-per-view event, and the NWO had become a federation within a federation.

The NWO gained more national attention when basketball superstar Dennis Rodman agreed to be in Team NWO's corner for its match against Team WCW for a three-way match at the Uncensored pay-per-view on March 16. Rodman was the perfect NWO celebrity: he didn't care what people thought about him.

Team NWO, consisting of Nash, Hall, Hogan, Dennis Rodman, and Randy Savage, won again. Their prize: the right to demand a shot at any WCW title whenever it wished.

The rise of the NWO had become wrestling's top story of 1997. At the same time, however, there were signs that the NWO was falling apart from within. Hogan took a brief vacation. So did Nash, leaving Hall to defend the world tag team title with Savage and Konnan as substitute partners. DiBiase started urging the NWO members to have more mercy on their opponents.

"We're just not united anymore," Nash said of the NWO.

United or not, the NWO had the wrestling world's attention as fans and the media anxiously awaited their next move. When it came, DiBiase was fired. Claiming that "tradition bites," Nash, Hall, and Syxx started feuding with WCW veterans Ric Flair and Roddy Piper.

Hall and Nash continued their feud with the Steiners, and cheated their way to one victory after another. Former world champion Curt Hennig defected from Flair's Four Horsemen to the NWO during a War Games cage match that saw Nash, Syxx, Konnan, and Marcus Bagwell defeat the Horsemen.

Nash was having the time of his life in WCW until he tore ligaments in his right knee during a card in Seattle on September 19, 1997. The injury kept him on the sidelines for three months. Nash could only sit and watch while Syxx—who took his place in world tag team title defenses—and Hall lost the belts to the Steiners less than a month later.

Meanwhile, Nash was having a running argument with The Giant, who had been a member of the NWO. At the World War III pay-per-view, Nash disguised himself as Sting and attacked The Giant with a baseball bat. They finally met in the ring at Souled Out on January 24, 1998, and Nash made sure he didn't lose by throwing hot coffee in The Giant's face. Then he powerbombed The Giant, giving him a concussion. As a result, WCW banned wrestlers from using the power bomb.

Amidst all this, Nash and Hall regained the tag team belts from the Steiners. A tumultuous several months followed. In early February, Nash and Hall again lost the belts to the Steiners. Two weeks later, they got them back when Scott turned against his brother.

Things started going wrong for the NWO. Nash and Hogan weren't getting along. The problems started when Bischoff fired Syxx, one of Nash's best friends. When Hogan said in an interview that Syxx wasn't good enough for the

NWO, Nash got even angrier. Nash got a shot against WCW World champion Sting at WCW's *Monday Nitro*, but he was disqualified when Hogan interfered. The NWO was in turmoil. Wrestling's most influential clique was coming apart at the seams.

Disaster struck at Spring Stampede '98, when Hogan and Nash teamed up against Piper and The Giant. During the match, Hogan accidentally—or so it seemed—struck Nash in the stomach with a baseball bat. When Hogan pinned Piper, Nash refused to raise his partner's hand. Hogan turned around and again bashed Nash with the bat.

The next night at *Nitro*, new WCW World champion Randy Savage put his belt on the line against Hogan. During the match, Nash powerbombed Hogan and declared that he was through with Hogan. Savage declared Nash the new leader of the NWO.

Now there were two NWOs: NWO Wolfpac, led by Nash, and NWO Hollywood, led by Hogan. Bischoff, who stayed with Hogan, put pressure on Hall to join NWO Hollywood. Hall declined. "Me and Kev are tighter than ever," he declared. "I'm NWO for life."

Just a week after declaring his lifelong friendship with Nash, Hall attacked his longtime friend at Slamboree '98. Hall and Nash were defending their tag team title against Sting and The Giant. With Nash about to pin The Giant, Hall hit Nash over the head with one of the championship belts. Hall then rolled The Giant on top of Nash for the pin. Not only had Hall given up his friendship with Nash, but he had given up the world tag team title. Nash was taken to the hospital and treated for a concussion, but the pain of being betrayed by his best friend was worse.

The sides were set. NWO Wolfpac: Nash, Savage, Luger, Sting, Hennig, and Konnan. NWO Hollywood: Hogan, Hall, and Dusty Rhodes.

At first, Hall and Nash refused to wrestle each other. Nash even ran into the ring to help Hall in a title match against Hogan, but he ended up getting attacked by Hall. Obviously, Hall had no interest in shaking hands and making up. Their hatred for each other intensified when Nash attacked Hall at *Nitro*, inciting a riot between members of NWO Hollywood and NWO Wolfpac. In a nine-man battle royal at Road Wild, Nash eliminated himself to get at Hall, who had just been eliminated by Bill Goldberg. They fought it out as if they had never been friends for a day.

While members of the Wolfpac and NWO Hollywood were asking other wrestlers, "Whose

Unable to get along with Hollywood Hogan, Kevin Nash formed a splinter NWO group called the Wolfpac, which included, from left to right: Lex Luger, Sting, Nash, Konnan, and, Randy Savage (who is not pictured).

side are you on?" there was no doubt whose side the fans were on: the Wolfpac's. Nash was a fan favorite once again.

The feud with Hall took an exhausting toll on Nash, who really wanted nothing less than to feud with his former friend. Hall, who had recently been arrested, was obviously drunk when he came to the ring for a match against Luger on September 14, 1998. When Nash tried to help him, Hall asked, "Where were you when my life was falling apart?" A few weeks later, Hall joined Stevie Ray in an attack on Nash. Nothing was off-limits. The Wolfpac smashed NWO Hollywood's limousine. Nash was ambushed by Hall in a bar. Hall and Nash had car chases through city streets.

Hall and Nash finally went face-to-face in the ring at Halloween Havoc '98. After flooring Hall with two devastating jackknifes, Nash simply walked away from the ring and allowed himself to get counted out. The next night at *Nitro*, Hall and The Giant ambushed Nash. The end of this feud was nowhere in sight, or so it seemed.

Nash still had winning the WCW World title on his mind, and he took a major step toward the belt when he dominated a battle royal in which the first prize was a match against world champion Bill Goldberg at Starrcade '98.

Starrcade '98, held on December 27, was a memorable night in Washington, D.C. The fans in the nation's capital saw Nash win his first WCW World title by pinning Goldberg in a match filled with controversy. Nash was on the mat and about to get pinned when Disco Inferno, who for months had been begging for entrance into the Wolfpac, ran into the ring.

Goldberg disposed of Inferno, then disposed of another interfering star, Bam Bam Bigelow.

Goldberg, who had never lost a match in his career of over one year, turned his attention back to Nash. Hall walked to ringside dressed as a security guard, grabbed Goldberg, shoved an electric cattle prod into his chest, and administered a current that sent Goldberg convulsing to the mat, where he was pinned by Nash.

Not only was Nash the new WCW World champion, but the Outsiders were back together again. On January 4, 1999, Nash lay down and allowed Hogan to pin him for the title. When Nash got up, he hugged Hogan, Hall, and Scott Steiner. Once again, there was only one NWO, and they made their presence known. Nash pinned Rey Misterio Jr., forcing the proud Mexican wrestler to remove the mask he had worn for his entire career. Misterio was tearful and felt humiliated.

Nash, Hall, and Hogan had a great time inside the ring and out. Highlight tapes of their weekly antics became a regular feature of *Nitro*. Nash found time to win his second WCW World title, defeating Dallas Page at Slamboree '99. Page was nearly disqualified when Savage interfered on his behalf, but Bischoff ordered the match to continue. When it did, Nash finished off Page with a thundering power bomb.

All of the calls were going in the NWO's favor, and Nash was becoming more popular than ever. He appeared on television talk shows such as *Live with Regis and Kathie Lee* and *The Tonight Show with Jay Leno*. On *The Tonight Show*, Nash challenged Bret Hart to a match, putting up $250,000 of his own money. Hart accepted the challenge, but the match never took place because of the untimely death of Owen Hart, Bret's brother.

At Bash at the Beach on July 11, 1999, Nash and Sting battled Savage and Sid Vicious in a tag team match with some unusual stipulations: not only was Nash's world title on the line, but anyone, including Sting, was eligible to beat him for the belt. Savage and his entourage, which included Gorgeous George, Madusa, and Miss Madness, were too much for Nash. Sting stung him with a "Stinger splash." Gorgeous George weakened him with two low blows. Finally, Savage put away the champion with a top-rope elbowsmash that hit its mark.

"Belts come and go," Nash said. "I know that as well as anyone. What bothers me more than losing the belt is how sneaky Sting has become.

At Slamboree '98, Scott Hall turned against his friend Kevin Nash, hitting him over the head with a WCW championship belt. The two feuded for a while, then mended their friendship and teamed up again.

If you want to know Sting's real colors, look at his back: it's yellow. Sting had a chance to prove that he was on my side tonight and he didn't do it. That's all I need to know."

The next night, Nash helped Hogan regain the title from Savage. Then he dropped a bomb: he wanted a title shot against Hogan.

Even though Hogan and Nash were on the same side, this wasn't such an outlandish request. Nash was still embarrassed about lying down for Hogan and giving up the belt in January, and he wanted a chance for retribution. Hogan, however, was stunned by Nash's request and took it personally.

Hogan and Nash had their showdown in a retirement match at the Road Wild pay-per-view on August 14 in Sturgis, North Dakota. More than the title was on the line—whoever lost would have to retire permanently.

For a while, it looked like that man would be Hogan. Nash floored Hogan with a devastating power bomb, but Hogan somehow managed to kick out before the three-count. Displaying the resiliency that had made him a champion throughout his career, Hogan rallied to pin Nash, retain the title, and send him into retirement.

"I'll be back," Nash promised. "Somehow I'll be back. I've seen Hogan manipulate the rules lots of times. There must be a loophole. I'll find it." As 1999 came to a close, Nash and Hall showed up at several WCW cards, but as audience members, not participants. The Outsiders were truly on the outside, but they insist they won't be there forever.

Chronology

1958   Born in Detroit, Michigan, on July 9

1990   Signs his first contract with the NWA and wrestles as Steel

1991   Wrestles as Oz in NWA/WCW, making his first appearance on May 19

1992   Changes his name to Vinnie Vegas and pins former world champion Tommy Rich at Clash of the Champions XVIII; joins "Diamond" Dallas Page's "Diamond Mine" stable

1993   Signs with the WWF and becomes Diesel, Shawn Michaels's bodyguard

1994   Wins his first WWF Intercontinental title from Razor Ramon at Wrestle-Mania X; teams with Michaels to win the WWF World tag team title from the Headshrinkers; loses the WWF Intercontinental title to Ramon; breaks with Michaels; wins his first WWF World heavyweight title from Bob Backlund

1995   Reunites with Michaels; loses the WWF World heavyweight title to Bret Hart at the Survivor Series; wins the WWF World tag team title with Michaels; loses the WWF World tag team title; voted Wrestler of the Year by the readers of *Pro Wrestling Illustrated*

1996   Leaves the WWF and signs with WCW, where he uses his real name, Kevin Nash; forms the Outsiders and the NWO with Scott Hall; wins the WCW World tag team title with Hall

1997   Loses the WCW World tag team title after being sidelined with a knee injury

1998   With Scott Hall, wins the WCW World tag team title from Rick and Scott Steiner; loses the belt to the Steiners 13 days later; regains the tag belt from the Steiners; loses the tag belts to The Giant and Sting; wins the WCW World heavyweight title at Starrcade '98 from Bill Goldberg

1999   Forfeits the WCW World heavyweight title to Hollywood Hogan; regains the WCW World heavyweight title from "Diamond" Dallas Page at Slamboree '99; loses the WCW World heavyweight title; loses a loser-must-retire match to Hulk Hogan at Road Wild

Further Reading

Basil, Dr. Sidney M. "Hall Is Crying Out for Nash's Friendship." *The Wrestler* (March 1999): 58–61.

Burkett, Harry. "Kevin Nash & Hollywood Hogan: the Untold Story of Why They Never Kliqued." *The Wrestler* (September 1998): 48–51.

"Far from the Spotlight, Kevin Nash—Champion Dad—Reigns." *The Wrestler Presents True Life Stories* (Winter 1998): 26–37.

Hunter, Matt. *The Story of the Wrestler They Call "Hollywood" Hulk Hogan.* Philadelphia: Chelsea House Publishers, 2000.

Hunter, Matt. *Superstars of Men's Pro Wrestling.* Philadelphia: Chelsea House Publishers, 1998.

"Q&A: Kevin Nash." *The Wrestler* (Holiday 1999), 20–23.

Rosenbaum, Dave. "Nash & Hall: Survey Says . . . They're Not Long for the NWO." *Wrestler Digest* (Fall 1998): 84–89.

Rosenbaum, Dave. "Sting: He's Going to Be a Pain in the Nash." *Wrestler Digest* (Summer 1999): 44–46.

Index

Photo Credits
All Star Sports: p. 55; AP/Wide World Photos: p. 16; Jeff Eisenberg Sports Photography: pp. 2, 6, 11, 14, 18, 20, 22, 25, 28, 31, 34, 38, 40, 43; Howard Kernats Photography: pp. 50, 58, 60; Sports Action: p. 48.

JACQUELINE MUDGE is a frequent contributor to sports and entertainment magazines in the United States. Born in Idaho, she became a wrestling fan at age 11 when her father took her to matches. Although she has a degree in journalism, she left the writing arena for several years in the late-1980s to pursue a career in advertising sales. She returned to the profession—and the sport she loves— in 1995. Her previously published volumes on the mat sport include *Randy Savage: The Story of the Wrestler They Call "Macho Man"* and *Bret Hart: The Story of the Wrestler They Call "The Hitman."*